Little Boy Blue

AND OTHER COLORFUL RHYMES

Illustrated by

KRISTA BRAUCKMANN-TOWNS

JANE CHAMBLESS WRIGHT

WENDY EDELSON

ANITA NELSON

LORI NELSON FIELD

DEBBIE PINKNEY

KAREN PRITCHETT

PUBLICATIONS INTERNATIONAL, LTD.

Little Boy Blue

Little Boy Blue,
Come, blow your horn.
The sheep's in the meadow,
The cow's in the corn.

Where's the little boy who
Looks after the sheep?
He's under the haystack
Fast asleep.

Gray Goose

Gray goose and gander,
Waft your wings together
And carry the king's daughter
Over the one-strand river.

Three Gray Geese

Three gray geese
    In a green field grazing;
Gray were the geese
    And green was the grazing.

Roses Are Red

Roses are red,
    Violets are blue,
Sugar is sweet,
    And so are you!

My Little Pink

My little Pink,
    I suppose you think
I cannot do without you.
    I'll let you know before I go,
How I will fare without you.

Blue Ribbon

If you love me, love me true,
  Send me a ribbon, and let it be blue;
If you do not, let it be seen,
  Send me a ribbon, a ribbon of green.

The Brown Owl

The brown owl sits in the ivy bush,
And she looks wondrous wise,
With a horny beak beneath her cowl,
And a pair of large round eyes.

Dressed in Blue

Those dressed in blue
Have loves true;
In green and white,
Forsaken quite.

Chook, Chook

Chook, chook, chook, chook, chook,
Good morning, Mrs. Hen.
How many chickens have you got?
Madam, I've got ten.
Four of them are yellow,
And four of them are brown,
And two of them are speckled red,
The nicest in the town.

Little Green House

There was a little green house,
  And in the little green house
There was a little brown house,
  And in the little brown house
There was a little yellow house,
  And in the little yellow house
There was a little white house,
  And in the little white house
There was a little heart.

Dapple Gray

I had a little hobby horse,
And it was dapple gray.
Its head was made of pea-straw,
Its tail was made of hay.

Jolly Red Nose

Nose, nose, jolly red nose,
And what gave you
that jolly red nose?
Nutmeg and ginger,
Cinnamon and cloves,
That's what gave me
This jolly red nose.